Success in English Writing

Barry Scholes
Anita Scholes
Stuart Bell
Series Editor: Jayne de Courcy

Ages 9–11 **BOOK 4**

Contents

Collins Educational
An Imprint of HarperCollinsPublishers

The ⭐3 Steps to Success ...

Step 1 — Key skills practice

★ *Success in English Book 4* provides practice in a number of important English Writing skills. These skills are the ones that your child needs to master in order to achieve a high level in the English National Test at the end of Key Stage 2. This book builds on the writing skills covered in *Success in English Book 2*.

★ Each chapter takes one writing skill and works through it in straightforward steps. At the end of each chapter there is a *Test yourself* section containing questions to answer. This allows you and your child to see how well the skill has been understood.

★ This in-depth teaching and practice ensures that your child achieves real understanding of each skill.

Step 2 — Practice with National Test questions

★ At the end of the book there is a *Writing Test* paper which is similar to the one that your child will have to sit in his/her KS2 English National Test.

★ This *Test* paper allows you to see the sort of passages and questions your child will meet in the Writing Test. The questions require your child to demonstrate most of the writing skills taught in the book.

★ Your child can do this Test paper immediately after working on the skills chapters. You might, however, prefer to wait and ask your child to do it a little later to check that the writing skills have been thoroughly mastered.

Step 3 — Improving your child's performance

★ The book contains detailed *Answers and Guidance* to the *Test yourself* sections. The authors, one of whom is a KS2 Test Examiner, provide model answers and explain what makes a good answer.

★ There is an easy-to-follow marking grid for the *Writing Test* paper which will help you to assess your child's writing. It explains what Test Examiners look for and what writing skills your child needs to demonstrate to raise their performance from a level 3 to a level 4 or level 5.

★ In this way, you can work with your child to help him/her improve his/her performance in the KS2 English National Test.

Help with timing

★ As the English National Test is timed, it is important that your child learns to answer questions within a time limit.

★ Each *Test yourself* section and the *Writing Test* paper give target times for answering the questions. If you choose to, you can ask your child to time himself/herself when answering the questions. You can then compare his/her time against the target times provided in the *Answers and Guidance*. In this way, you will form a good idea of whether your child is working at the right rate to complete the National Test Writing paper successfully.

Progression

★ *Success in English* is aimed at 9–11 year-olds who are in Years 5 and 6 of primary school. There is in-built progression: each book builds on skills taught in previous books.

★ To get the most out of *Success in English*, it is important that your child works through all four books in sequence. If you are buying this series for your child who is aged 9/10 (Year 5), then buy Books 1 and 2, and Books 3 and 4 at age 10/11 (Year 6). If your child is already in Year 6, then it is still advisable to work through from Book 1 to Book 4, to ensure that your child benefits from the progression built into the series.

Note to teachers

★ This book, and the other titles in the *Success in English* series, are designed for use at home and in schools in Years 5 and 6. They focus on the key reading and writing skills that will raise children's performance in the English National Test.

★ You can use the books in class or give them to children for homework to ensure that they are fully prepared for their English National Test.

1 Beginnings and endings

What's it all about?

★ In this chapter you will learn more about beginning and ending a story (which we also covered in Book 2).

★ You will learn how to begin a story with speech, and how to handle surprise endings.

★ In your National Test Writing paper, you will be expected to write a story that has a good beginning and an effective ending.

How to begin with speech

Many stories begin with speech, or conversation.
This is one example:

"That's odd," said Eleanor.

"What is?" asked Ben, as he joined his sister at the window.

"That man there, passing the Jennings' house."

"Seems ordinary enough to me," commented Ben.

"Look at the Jennings' dog. Have you ever known that dog not to bark its head off when anyone passes the gate?"

"No, never," Ben agreed. "I wonder who that chap is."

"Well, we're soon going to find out, because he's heading for our gate."

A good beginning to your story will hook your reader from the first few lines. The example above does it by using speech. The words "That's odd" immediately make us curious. As we read on, we learn what it is that is odd. The speech does other things too: it introduces the characters and describes the action.

How to handle a surprise ending

How you make your readers feel at the *end* of a story is very important. A story which ends in a way your readers expect, may leave them feeling disappointed. A surprise ending to a story can be very effective.

Here is a story plan with two different endings. Which do you think works best?

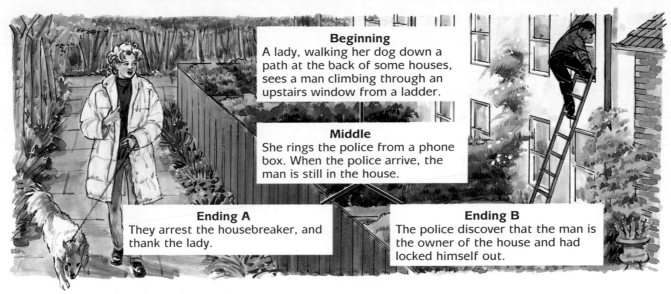

Beginning
A lady, walking her dog down a path at the back of some houses, sees a man climbing through an upstairs window from a ladder.

Middle
She rings the police from a phone box. When the police arrive, the man is still in the house.

Ending A
They arrest the housebreaker, and thank the lady.

Ending B
The police discover that the man is the owner of the house and had locked himself out.

Ending **A** is the one most readers will expect, but because you know it is coming it is disappointing. Ending **B** is a surprise, and so makes a more effective ending to the story.

Test yourself

1 Write the beginning to a story called 'Finders Keepers' using speech. Use the speech to 'hook' your reader, to introduce the characters and to describe the action. Try to write about 80 words.

2 This is part of a story plan for a story called 'In The Graveyard'. Write your own surprise ending to it. Try to write about 150 words. Make sure that your ending follows on from the events of the beginning and middle.

Beginning

Jason boasts about taking a short cut home every evening through a graveyard, and never being the slightest bit frightened. Two other children plan to play a trick on him.

Middle

They record ghostly noises on a portable tape recorder, intending to play it back behind a headstone as he passes by.

Answers and Guidance are given on p.34. **How long did you take?**

2 Describing the setting

★ In this chapter you will learn how to create atmosphere when you describe a setting.

★ You will learn to do this by choosing your words carefully and by using thoughts and feelings as part of the description.

How to create atmosphere

The atmosphere of a setting is its mood. Creating atmosphere means making your readers not only see your setting in their imagination, but also *feel* its mood.

As you read the following description, ask yourself how the writer has created atmosphere.

Although there was a faint smell of smoke, the house seemed to have escaped the terrible fire. Then, as the moon slid like a ghost from behind a cloud, I saw the black skeleton of roof beams. The walls above each empty window were stained with smoke. Broken glass glittered in the moonlight. I stood completely still in the garden, unable to believe my home was just an empty shell.

The writer creates atmosphere by his choice of language, and by describing the thoughts and feelings of the narrator. First the writer describes the scene in terms of what can be smelt and seen: the 'smell of smoke', 'the black skeleton of roof beams'. Then the writer uses words such as 'ghost' and 'skeleton' to make the scene seem frightening. Finally, the writer describes the reaction of the person telling the story: 'I stood completely still in the garden, unable to believe my home was just an empty shell.'

The writer uses a variety of special effects:

- **Powerful words**: e.g. 'glittered' (rather than 'burnt' or 'shone').

- **Similes** (saying one thing is like another): e.g. 'the moon slid like a ghost'.

- **Metaphors** (a way of comparing things by saying something is something else): e.g. a *skeleton* of roof beams.

Using some, or all, of these special effects in your own writing will help you to create atmosphere and bring your descriptions to life. Don't overdo it, though, or it will have the opposite effect. There is more about similes and metaphors in Chapter 12.

Test yourself

1. Use this picture to help you write a description of a carnival.

   First make lists or a plan of the following things to include in your description:

   - the sights, sounds, smells and tastes you might experience if you were there;
   - your thoughts and feelings;
   - powerful words, similes and metaphors to bring your description to life, and create atmosphere.

   Try to write about 80 words.

2. Write six or seven sentences describing a place you know well. First think of the atmosphere you want to create. Is it a happy or depressing place? Is it peaceful or noisy? Is it mysterious? Or does it have some other atmosphere? Make similar lists to those suggested in question **1** to help you plan your writing.

Answers and Guidance are given on p.34. **How long did you take?**

3 Creating believable characters

What's it all about?

★ In this chapter you will learn how to write about the thoughts and feelings of characters in your story.

★ You will learn how to 'get inside' your characters so that your reader can understand why they behave in the way they do.

★ In your National Test Writing paper, you will be expected to create believable characters.

Description

You may directly tell your readers what kind of person a character is. For example, you may say that he is selfish, clever, lazy or brave. A much better way is to let your readers discover this for themselves from the way the character behaves:

> Nick looked in the mirror as he passed. He smiled when he saw his clean white trainers and smart blue tracksuit.

This tells us that Nick is neat and tidy, *and* suggests he is vain.

Thoughts and feelings

You also need to tell your readers what your character is thinking and feeling:

> Nick was now a metre ahead of Amran, and for the first time he knew he could win the race. He felt a thrill run through him. He would be the winner, the hero of the day and the centre of attention.

Reasons for behaviour

Once your readers know what kind of person a character is, and what he/she thinks and feels, they will be able to understand why the character behaves in that way:

> With just six metres to go, Nick stumbled and fell. By the time he had scrambled to his feet, the last runner was already crossing the finishing line. Then someone in the crowd began to laugh and point at him. Others began to laugh too.

"Just look at Smarty Pants!" jeered one of them.

Nick's running kit was smeared with mud, his face was just as dirty and his hair was a mess. Nick felt he had to get out of there as quickly as possible. He raced off the field and into the changing room. As he did so, tears ran down his cheeks, streaking his muddy face.

We understand why Nick ran away crying. The writer has shown how proud he was of his appearance, and how sure he was that everyone would admire him if he won the race. Losing the race, being called 'Smarty Pants', and having his smart appearance totally messed up, were too much for Nick to bear.

Test yourself

Session 1

1 Write a paragraph, of about six or seven sentences, telling about the meeting between this timid boy and the dog. Tell your reader what kind of person he is, what he does and what he is thinking and feeling.

2 What is this girl thinking and feeling about the other two characters? Write a few sentences which tell about her thoughts and feelings.

 How long did you take?

Session 2

3 Why do you think this character is behaving in the way he is? Write three short paragraphs about him. Use all three ways described above to allow your readers to 'get inside' him.

Paragraph 1: Tell your reader what the boy looks like. Find a way of suggesting what kind of person he is, without saying so directly.

Paragraph 2: Say what he is thinking and feeling.

Paragraph 3: Describe what the boy does in the end. Make sure that your reader will understand why he behaves the way he does.

 How long did you take?

Answers and Guidance are given on p.35.

4 Using speech

What's it all about?

★ In this chapter you will learn how to use speech (dialogue) to show what your characters are like, and to move your plot along.

★ In your National Test Writing paper, you will be awarded extra marks if you use speech well.

How to write speech

You can use speech (dialogue) to show your readers what your characters are thinking and feeling, and how they react to each other. When your characters talk to each other, they can also move your plot along by discussing things that have happened.

Read this conversation:

"Hi, Alice. What are you looking so glum about?"

"Hi, Emma. I've just had a row with Mum."

"What about?" asked her friend.

"My room. It all started when she said she was sick of the mess and I should tidy it up."

"And you didn't," guessed Emma.

"No. And then she came in and tidied it up when I was at school."

"Great! Saved you a job."

"No, you don't understand. Mum and I had an agreement. She'd keep out of my room if I kept it tidy."

"But you didn't," pointed out Emma.

"No. But she never gave me a final warning, did she? She just went in and turned everything upside down. And then she found my diary."

"She read it?" asked Emma in astonishment.

"I don't know," replied Alice, looking gloomier than ever. "I think so. I hope not."

"There's something you don't want her to know about?"

"Yes."

"Tell me more," encouraged Emma.

The conversation tells us a lot about the two girls. We know what Alice thinks and feels about her mum tidying her room, and what she is afraid of. We know from the way Emma reacts that she is surprised by what has happened and is very curious about what is in Alice's diary. This conversation also tells us quite a lot about what happened at Alice's home.

Notice how the writer makes every word of the conversation count. Each line of speech tells us something important about what has happened, and often gives clues to understanding the character.

Notice also that the writer does not need to say 'said Alice' or 'asked Emma' every time a person speaks, because the conversation makes clear who is speaking. The writer does, however, occasionally refer to the speaker's name to make it absolutely clear.

Look at the way speech marks have been used. There is more about this in Chapter 13.

Test yourself

Session 1

1 Write a conversation (of about 150 words) between two children who see a mysterious box floating in a canal. Find ways to make sure that your speech reveals the characters and helps move your story along.

How long did you take?

Session 2

2 Write the beginning to a story called 'Muddy Footprints'. Begin with a conversation which introduces the characters and tells us about their thoughts and feelings. Try to write about 150 words. Make every word count.

How long did you take?

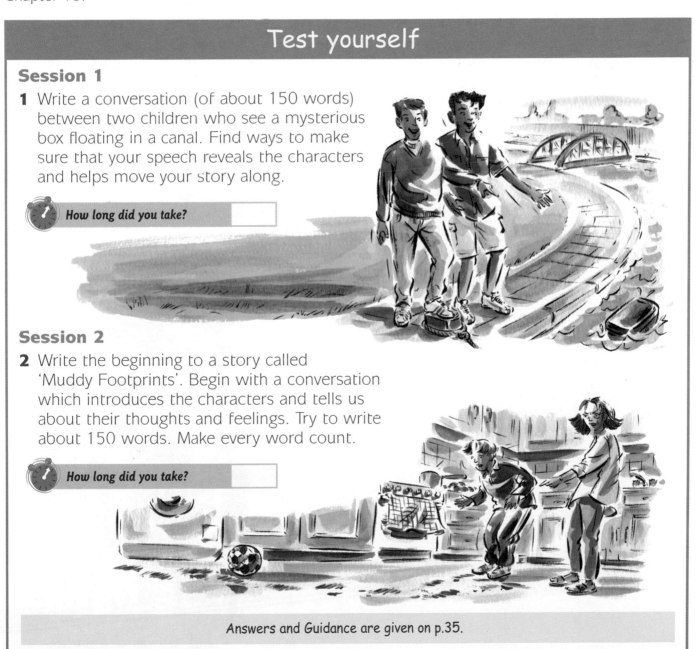

Answers and Guidance are given on p.35.

5 A recipe for a story

| What's it all about? | ★ In this chapter you will learn how to mix narrative, description and speech successfully in your stories. |
| | ★ If you choose to write a story in your National Test Writing paper, the examiners will assess how well you can do this. |

Getting the right mix

You already know that your story needs a plot – a sequence of events that unfolds through the story. You also know that these events need to be organised into a clear beginning, middle and end.

When you write about these events, you are using **narrative**. But narrative on its own does not make a gripping story. To really hold the interest of your reader, you need to think about how you can mix narrative with other story ingredients.

The three main ingredients of a good story are:

● narrative

● description

● speech.

You need to mix these three up in the right way so that they add variety to your story. At the same time, you want to make sure your plot moves along fast enough to hold your reader's attention.

Read these two versions of the same story.

A

Two girls were standing at the top of a hill, looking down the road for their friend Jo.

Laura thought their friend would not come, but Charly suggested they wait another ten minutes. Laura decided they should go back and look for her.

They free-wheeled down the hill on their bikes. About halfway down, Laura spotted something which brought them skidding to a stop. It was Jo's bike lying on the grass verge, but there was no sign of Jo. A metre or so beyond it there was a steep drop into the valley.

At that moment they heard a faint cry.

B

"I don't think she's coming," said Laura. She was standing at the top of a hill, her long dark hair blowing across her face. Far below in the valley was the village of Dunbury, but there was no sign of Jo on the road.

"Let's give her another ten minutes," suggested her friend. Charly was taller than Laura, with short fair hair, but both girls were dressed in jeans and T-shirts.

"I think we should go back and look for her," replied Laura. "It's not like Jo to be late."

They free-wheeled down the hill on their bikes. About halfway down, Laura suddenly cried, "Look!" Jo's bike was lying on the grass verge. They skidded to a stop, but there was no sign of Jo. A metre or so beyond it, there was a steep drop into the valley.

At that moment they heard a faint cry.

Version **A** is all narrative. There is one action, or event, after another. There is no description and no speech.

Version **B** mixes narrative, description and speech very successfully, without interrupting the action. The opening conversation takes us straight into the story. All the important descriptive details of setting and character are given, but only when the reader needs them. The conversation explains the girls' problem, without wasting any words, and keeps the narrative flowing.

Test yourself

Session 1

1 The beginning of this story is all narrative. Rewrite it, mixing in speech and description in such a way that the flow of the story is not interrupted. Try to write about 150 words.

Nick and Tony were walking home from school. They passed a house with a high fence. Suddenly they heard children's laughter from behind the fence. They wondered what was going on, but there was no crack or hole in the fence to peep through. Then Tony noticed a hole above their heads. He asked Nick to let him climb on his shoulders so he could look through. Peeping through, he could see two children swimming in a pool. They were really enjoying themselves. Nick asked what Tony could see, but Tony told him to keep quiet, in case the children heard him.

 How long did you take?

Session 2

2 Write your own beginning to a story called 'Locked Out'. Mix speech and description with the narrative. Try to write about 150 words.

 How long did you take?

Answers and Guidance are given on p.36.

13

What's it all about?

★ In this chapter you will learn how to choose a narrator for your story.

★ You will also learn the importance of writing your story in a suitable form, as this will gain you extra marks in your National Test Writing paper.

Choosing a narrator

A story can be told by the writer in the **third person**:

> As <u>Tanya</u> left the park <u>she</u> heard a shout from up the street.

Or it can be told from the point of view of the main character, writing in the **first person**:

> As <u>I</u> left the park <u>I</u> heard a shout from up the street.

If you decide that the main character is going to tell the story, you need to use his or her words to tell us what kind of person he/she is. Read this story opening. What does it tell us about the main character?

"Roy!"

I hate that name, but there's not much I can do about it. You're just given your name. It's probably the most important and personal thing you own, and nobody gives you a choice.

I pretended I hadn't heard and turned over in bed.

"Roy, it's time to get up!"

What I'd like to know is this: why do I have to go to bed when I'm wide awake, but get up when I'm tired? I rolled out of bed and caught sight of myself in the mirror. When I saw a mousey-haired, bleary-eyed eleven-year-old looking back at me, I wished I hadn't.

We can tell from this opening that Roy is a lazy, mousey-haired eleven-year-old, who is not happy with the way adults run his life. He hates his name and is not particularly pleased with his appearance.

Whether you choose to write your story in the third person or the first person, you must be consistent and use the same narrator (or narrative voice) the whole way through.

Choosing a suitable narrative form

In your National Test Writing paper, you will be given a choice of two stories to write. Each will have a heading. Sometimes you may be given the first line or the last line. All these things should help you to choose a suitable form for your story. Look at these titles:

'Lost and Found' – this title suggests that the story should be in the form of an adventure or mystery.
'The fun was just beginning.' This first line suggests a funny story.
'When I landed back on Earth, I promised myself I would never take a lift in a spacecraft again.' This last line could suggest a science-fiction story or an adventure story.

Test yourself

Session 1

1 Use this picture to help you write the beginning to a story called 'A Fear of Spiders'. Write from the point of view of the main character. Make sure you tell your reader her name, what kind of person she is, and what she thinks and feels about what happens. Try to write about 120–130 words.

 How long did you take?

Session 2

2 Use this picture to help you write the beginning to a story called 'Time Travellers'. Choose an appropriate form for your story. Try to write about 120 words.

 How long did you take?

Answers and Guidance are given on p.36.

What's it all about?

⭐ In this chapter you will learn how to organise your work into paragraphs, and how to use headings and sub-headings.

⭐ In your National Test Writing paper, you will gain marks for good layout and organisation of your writing.

How to organise ideas in paragraphs

You have already learned how to use paragraphs in developing your stories. In this chapter you will learn how to use a paragraph for each main idea in your information writing.

The paragraph below is a group of sentences about the same main idea. The first sentence introduces the main idea, while the other sentences support it by giving more detail.

Some people think zoos are cruel. They don't like seeing animals behind bars. They prefer to see them in wildlife parks where they have more space.

Mark was asked by his teacher to write a page on lions for a brochure that a zoo gives out to visitors. He researched the information and then decided to organise it into four paragraphs. See if you can decide what the main idea is for each one.

Lions are tawny yellow in colour, which helps them blend into their surroundings. The male lion is heavier than the female and has a mane. It may be over two metres long, nearly a metre high at the shoulder, and weigh over 200 kilograms.

Lions are found in Africa and in the Gir wildlife santuary in India. They live in groups called prides on open grassy plains or bush country. They defend their own territory from other lions.

The lioness does most of the hunting. Lions feed on a variety of grazing animals, such as antelope or zebra. They are sometimes killed when attacking buffalo.

A lioness may give birth to three or four cubs.

Headings and sub-headings

Headings and sub-headings are signposts to help your reader find his or her way around your writing. The main heading says what the writing as a whole is about. Each paragraph may then have a sub-heading which tells what its main idea is.

Here is a list of a main heading and four sub-headings for the text about lions. See if you can pick out the main heading, and then match each sub-heading to its correct paragraph.

What they eat
Their young
Where they live
The life of lions
What they look like

The main heading is **The life of lions** because that is what the writing is about. The remaining paragraphs should have these sub-headings:

Paragraph 1 – **What they look like**
Paragraph 2 – **Where they live**
Paragraph 3 – **What they eat**
Paragraph 4 – **Their young**.

Test yourself

Session 1

1 Using the same sub-headings as for lions, organise a piece of writing about any living creature of your choice. Choose a main heading to suit your subject. Write a short paragraph for each sub-heading.

 How long did you take?

Session 2

2 Choose a subject you know quite a lot about, such as a hobby or a favourite sport, and write three or four paragraphs about it. Write a plan for your work, with suitable headings and sub-headings to show the main ideas.

 How long did you take?

Answers and Guidance are given on p.37.

8 Different ways to organise your writing

Purpose

Why you are writing is known as the **purpose** of your writing. The purpose will affect the way your writing is organised. For example, you will need to organise instructions differently from a letter, or from a leaflet persuading someone about something.

Audience

Who you are writing for is your **audience** (your readers). The way you write will change according to your audience. For example, if you write an explanation for younger readers, you will need to use simple words and short sentences. In an explanation for older children or adults, you can use more formal language.

How to write a leaflet

Leaflets are often written to persuade someone about something. Think about *why* this single-page leaflet has been written, and *who* it has been written for?

SAVE OUR SCHOOL!

Main heading: the campaign slogan

Bloggstown Council wants to close Greenbank Primary School, because of falling numbers. Instead they want the children to travel over three miles to Brick View School, in the centre of busy Bloggstown.

Short explanation of the issue

Why Greenbank must not close

- A new estate is being built close by, and there will soon be lots of new pupils at Greenbank.
- Our exam results are much better than those of Brick View.
- Brick View School is over three miles away on very busy roads.
- The area around Greenbank is excellent for nature study and other outdoor activities.
- The area around Brick View School is built up.
- We have the best school sports field in the town.

Main points set out clearly

Do not let them take away our school. Protest now to Bloggstown Council.

Conclusion: urging people to take action

Session 1

1 Write a single-page leaflet about protecting a local park or green space from vandals and other thoughtless behaviour.

- Think about *why* you are writing.
- Think about *who* you are writing for: young children, older children or adults? Think about how you can present your leaflet so that your intended audience will want to read it and learn the important facts.
- Make notes of what you want to say, and why you think so. Make sure you have listed all the important points.
- Plan your leaflet with the following:
  - an eye-catching slogan
  - a short explanation of why the space needs protecting
  - a list of your main points set out clearly
  - and a short conclusion.
- Design and illustrate your leaflet, if you want to.

 How long did you take?

Session 2

2 Use this information about firework safety to write a leaflet **aimed at 5–8 year olds**. If you like, you can illustrate your leaflet so that it will be eye-catching to young children.

Fireworks must be kept in a closed box and it's a good idea to keep them in a locked cupboard until you want to use them. Grown-ups should only take one firework out at a time and must close the box each time in case a spark from a lit firework sets the others off. Only adults should light fireworks. Everyone watching should stand a long way back from where the fireworks are being lit. No one should ever go back to a firework once it has been lit. You should never throw fireworks. You should never put fireworks in your pocket. You should keep pets indoors.

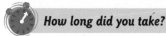 *How long did you take?*

Answers and Guidance are given on p.37.

| What's it all about? | ★ In this chapter you will learn how to make sure you cover all the important points in your writing. |
| | ★ You will also learn how to plan and organise a letter. |

How to cover the important points

Look at how the plan below for a letter about a school trip uses headings and sub-headings to organise the important points.

Letters don't have headings and sub-headings but it's still a good idea to use these when planning what you want to write and how to organise it. This will help you not to miss anything out.

LETTER PLAN

Time and date of trip

Thursday 12th June, 9.00 am to 6.00 pm.

Purpose of trip

To help us with our 'water' project.

Transport

Coach

Where we're going and what we're doing

To Malham. Walk from car park to Malham Cove. Packed lunch at Cove. Afternoon walk to Malham Tarn. Coach pick up at tarn 4.00 pm.

Cost

£5 each, to be brought in as soon as possible.

Clothing required

Waterproof coat, walking boots or stout shoes, backpack.

Food

Packed lunch.

Permissions slip

To be filled in by 9th May.

Test yourself

Session 1

1 Use the plan opposite to write a letter telling parents about the school trip it describes. (If you prefer, you may write about an actual school trip that you have done.) Don't forget to begin and end your letter correctly.

 How long did you take?

Session 2

2 Make a *plan* for a brochure about your school to welcome new pupils and their parents. First make a list of the headings you will use in the brochure. Then make notes of all the important points which you will put under those headings. Two of the headings you will need are: School hours, Uniform.

 How long did you take?

Session 3

3 Write a list of instructions for making a favourite food or drink. Organise your instructions under these headings: Equipment, Ingredients, Method.

 How long did you take?

Answers and Guidance are given on p.38.

10 Writing a good conclusion

What's it all about?

⭐ In this chapter you will learn how to shape your informative writing so that it ends well.

⭐ In your National Test Writing paper, the examiners will award marks for a well-written final paragraph.

How to write a good conclusion

Different types of writing need different sorts of conclusion:

Type 1

If your writing is trying to **persuade** your reader about something, then your final paragraph will need to ask your reader to do something. Look back at Chapter 8 (p.18) to see how the writer of the 'Save Our School!' leaflet ends by urging readers to take action.

Type 2

If you are writing an **explanation** about something, you will be covering a number of different points. Your conclusion should be a summary of the most important points – this means going back *briefly* over them.

These are the planning notes for a piece of writing Patrick did on 'Why I like fishing'. Note how he has underlined the most important points and summarised them in his conclusion.

> Why I like fishing
> Gets you out of doors
> Peace and quiet
> <u>Make new friends</u>
> Choosing the right bait and float to tempt a fish
> <u>The excitement of catching and reeling in a fish</u>
> <u>Talking about it afterwards</u>
> Sometimes eating the fish

His final paragraph sums up the main points:

> I have made a lot of new friends since I started fishing. The most exciting part of my hobby is reeling in a fish, but talking about it afterwards to friends is almost as much fun!

Type 3

If your writing looks at two sides of an issue, the best way to end it is to give your own *opinion*.

Florence has already written a first paragraph listing the good points of her new school. Her second paragraph says what she is not too keen on. Her final paragraph summarises the main points and gives her opinion:

> I think my new school has more to offer than my old one: bigger classrooms and lots of clubs. Although I miss singing in the choir and my old school friends, I am sure I will make new friends very soon.

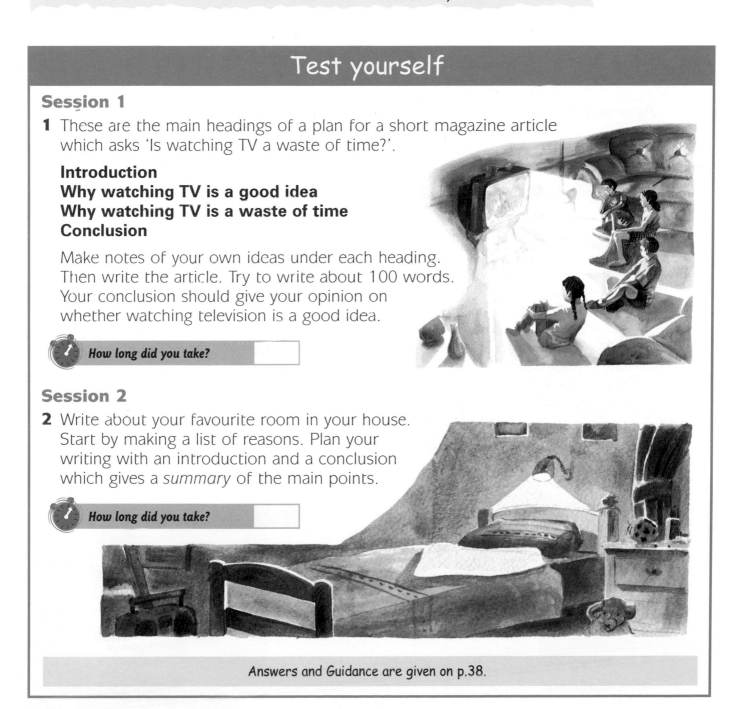

Test yourself

Session 1

1 These are the main headings of a plan for a short magazine article which asks 'Is watching TV a waste of time?'.

Introduction
Why watching TV is a good idea
Why watching TV is a waste of time
Conclusion

Make notes of your own ideas under each heading. Then write the article. Try to write about 100 words. Your conclusion should give your opinion on whether watching television is a good idea.

How long did you take?

Session 2

2 Write about your favourite room in your house. Start by making a list of reasons. Plan your writing with an introduction and a conclusion which gives a *summary* of the main points.

How long did you take?

Answers and Guidance are given on p.38.

11 Choosing the right language

How to choose the right language

Different kinds of writing need different language. Read these two accounts of the same event, both written by Rachel. The first is part of a report about a school trip for her school magazine. The second is part of a letter about the same trip to her friend. Why do you think Rachel uses different language?

Account A

On the 12th of June we left school by coach on a cold, but dry day. We arrived at Malham in the Yorkshire Dales just before 11 a.m. We then walked about a mile and a half from the village to Malham Cove. The cove is a sheer, overhanging wall of limestone almost 100 metres high. It is popular with rock climbers. Water flows from underground at the foot of the cove, to join the River Aire. This water once used to flow in a valley above the cove, but now finds its way underground through the limestone. A steep stony path leads to the top of the cove. Here there is a limestone pavement, with narrow fissures (cracks) where small flowers and ferns grow.

Account B

Dear Mel,

Yesterday we went to Malham on a school trip. The weather was cold and miserable and so was I. Why they put the coach park at one end of the village with the cove a mile and half away at the other end I'll never know. Malham Cove is just a big cliff of limestone, but we had fun watching the rock climbers. Another interesting thing was the underground stream that comes out at the bottom of the cove. The water was freezing!

Your choice of language will depend on three things:

● the **type** of text you are writing

● its **purpose**

● its **audience**.

We have covered all of these things in Chapters 8 and 9.

Let's now look at Rachel's writing again with these three things in mind.

Account A

Type of text
This is a report of the trip for the school magazine.

Purpose
Rachel has written it to *inform* people, so it deals with facts rather than opinions. It includes some technical words, such as 'limestone pavement' and 'fissures', so that people will see how much she has learnt from the trip.

Audience
She has written for children, teachers and parents so the language is quite formal.

Account B

Type of text
This is a personal letter.

Purpose
As Rachel is writing this letter to tell her friend what she thought about the trip, she can say what she liked and disliked, and doesn't need to use technical words.

Audience
As she is writing to a friend, she can write in a chatty, informal style.

Test yourself

Session 1

1 Write a short report for your school magazine of a recent school trip, sports match or concert. Try to write about 100 words. Match your choice of language to this type of writing. Think about *purpose* and *audience*.

2 Write a letter to a friend about the same event. Again match your choice of language to this type of writing, its purpose and audience.

 How long did you take?

Session 2

3 Write a paragraph describing your school for an article on 'Local buildings' in the local newspaper. Describe the building and the grounds.

4 Write the opening paragraph to an exciting story which has your school as its setting. Decide for yourself which details you will use to describe the setting.

 How long did you take?

Answers and Guidance are given on p.39.

12 Using similes and metaphors

What's it all about?

★ In this chapter you will learn how to use similes and metaphors well.

★ In your National Test Writing paper, you may gain marks if you use these well in your writing.

Similes

If you compare an object to something else, you are using a **simile**. Similes contain the words 'like' or 'as'. There are many similes which people use often:

as strong as an ox   as slow as a tortoise   like greased lightning

Such similes are so well-known that we don't really think about them, so they are not as effective as they once were. To create a strong picture in the mind of your reader, you will need to find new ways to use similes, like these:

My bedroom is so cold it's like the inside of an iceberg.

The wind raced along the street like an express train.

His face was as battered as an old tree trunk.

Metaphors

A **metaphor** is an unusual way of describing something. It is different from a simile because it does not use the words 'like' or 'as'.

Her feet were <u>like</u> blocks of ice   is a simile.

Her feet <u>were</u> blocks of ice   is a metaphor.

To make your writing fresh and clear always look for new ways of using metaphors, like this:

My brother tells so many jokes he is a joke machine.

Using similes and metaphors well

Read these two descriptions of Uncle John:

A

My Uncle John is a big man. He has a loud voice, and eyes which never miss anything. He won't stand any nonsense either. When he asks you to do something, you do it!

B

My Uncle John is a mountain of a man. He has a loud voice, and his eyes are as sharp as an eagle's. He won't stand any nonsense either. When he asks you to do something, you do it!

Version B gives the clearest picture of Uncle John because it uses a well-chosen metaphor and simile. Be careful not to use too many similes and metaphors in your writing. Just one or two well-chosen ones work best.

Test yourself

1 Say whether these are similes or metaphors.

   a Gareth was green with envy.

   b The sun was like a red balloon.

   c The moon was a misty ghost.

   d He is as slippery as an eel.

   e Her shop is a little gold mine.

   f Time flies.

   g The lake was like a mirror.

   h He is as tall as a tree.

2 Complete these sentences with suitable similes or metaphors of your own.

   a Clouds raced across the sky like _____.

   b The stone statue was _____ in the moonlight.

   c The wind tore at his clothes like _____.

   d In winter the house is _____.

   e Getting my brother to change his mind is like _____.

   f When it comes to remembering things my sister is _____.

3 Write two or three sentences about this picture. Use no more than two carefully chosen similes or metaphors to make your description clear and interesting.

Answers and Guidance are given on p.39. **How long did you take?**

13 Punctuating speech

What's it all about?

★ In this chapter you will learn how to use speech marks and other punctuation when you write dialogue.

★ In your National Test Writing paper, you will be expected to punctuate speech correctly.

How to use speech marks

Cartoons show spoken words inside a speech bubble:

In stories, spoken words are put inside speech marks:

" goes before the first word spoken

" goes after the last word spoken.

> The patient said, "Doctor, I'm turning into a dustbin!"
> "What rubbish!" replied the doctor.

Think of speech marks as 66 and 99.

How to punctuate speech

Look at how speech marks and other punctuation are used in this conversation:

> "OK, who's taken my bag?" asked Shelley. "I left it right here on the table."
>
> "It wasn't there when I came in," said Daljit. "What colour is it?"
>
> "It's red leather," replied Shelley, "and it's got all my school books in it."
>
> "I saw Katy with one just like that!" exclaimed Reeta.
>
> "Where was that, then?" asked Shelley.
>
> "She was leaving this room," Reeta told her. She thought for a moment, and then said, "About five minutes ago."

From the passage above we can find several rules for punctuating speech:

- Put " before the first spoken word.
- Begin the first spoken word with a capital letter.
- Put a comma, full stop, question mark or exclamation mark after the last spoken word.
- Put " to show the spoken words have ended.
- Words such as 'she said' may come before, after, or in the middle of the spoken words. Use commas to separate the spoken words from the rest of the sentence.
- Begin a new line for each speaker.

Session 1

1 Put these spoken words into sentences, using speech marks and any
other necessary punctuation.

2 Write two jokes of your own, using speech marks.

3 Rewrite this conversation using speech marks and other punctuation.
Remember to begin a new line for each speaker.

MOTHER	Ben, help Dad with the washing up.
BEN	But, Mum, it's Carly's turn today.
MOTHER	Carly, as you well know, has got to go back to school.
BEN	But, I did the dishes last night, and tomorrow night Carly is going to Auntie Helen's for tea.
MOTHER	Then she'll have wash the dishes two nights running.
BEN	It'll be three nights running.
MOTHER (*puzzled*)	Will it? I'll have to think about that one. Now help your dad.
DAD (*from the kitchen*)	It's all right. I've finished.

 How long did you take?

Session 2

4 Write the dialogue which might take place between
these people. Try to write about 10–12 lines.
Use speech marks and other necessary punctuation.

 How long did you take?

Answers and Guidance are given on p.40.

14 More punctuation

What's it all about?

★ In this chapter you will learn how to use the apostrophe, the colon, dashes and brackets.

★ In your National Test Writing paper, you may need to use these.

The apostrophe (')

The apostrophe is used in two ways:

● to show that something belongs to someone *or*

● to show that letters have been missed out of a word.

The apostrophe showing possession

the girl's books
(the books of the girl)

the lady's dresses
(the dresses of the lady)

the girls' bags
(the bags of the girls)

the ladies' dresses
(the dresses of the ladies)

You should not find it difficult to place the apostrophe correctly. First ask yourself who the owner is. Then put the apostrophe immediately after the owner or owners:

the bike of the boy – **the boy's bike**   the shoes of the boys – **the boys' shoes**

The apostrophe showing missing letters

Where words are shortened, the apostrophe shows where the missing letters are:

can't (cannot)   I'll (I will)   he's (he is)   they're (they are)   o'clock (of the clock)

The colon (:)

The colon is usually used to show that some kind of explanation or a list is to follow.

He refused to go: a blizzard was forecast.

The winners were: Jake Timms, Amy Gregson, Samantha Pearce and Jake Sampson.

Notice the use of commas to separate items in a list introduced by a colon.

Dashes

Dashes are used to show a sudden change of thought:

Bring me some crisps – no, make that an ice cream!

Another use is to show a strong idea added to a sentence:

Jenny says – and I really must agree with her – that the show was terrible.

Brackets

Brackets are used around words in a sentence to explain something:

The hero of the match (my brother) was cheered loudly by the crowd.

Or they may show an afterthought:

Tom slammed the door (as usual).

Test yourself

1 Change these expressions by using an apostrophe to show possession. Then use each new expression in a sentence of your own.

   a the hammer belonging to the man

   b the car belonging to Ms Smith

   c the coats of the girls

   d the cars belonging to the drivers

   e the brushes of the painters

   f the pens of the girl

2 Put each of these into its shortened form, and use it in a sentence of your own.

   a should not   **d** it is

   b we are   **e** they have

   c you will   **f** will not

3 Write two sentences with a colon: one to show items in a list; the other to show an explanation of the first part of the sentence.

4 Write two sentences which use dashes: one to show a sudden change of thought; the other to show a strong additional idea.

5 Write two sentences of your own using brackets: one to explain something; the other to show an afterthought.

Answers and Guidance are given on p.40. *How long did you take?*

15 Making sentences more interesting

What's it all about?

★ In this chapter you will learn how to make simple sentences more interesting by adding extra information.

★ In your National Test Writing paper, you will gain marks if you use a variety of interesting sentences.

Phrases

A **phrase** is a group of words which does not make complete sense on its own. It has no verb.

with the green fence   near the shed   with great difficulty

Phrases can be used to extend simple sentences, making them more interesting.
Adjective phrases add information about nouns:

The house <u>with the green fence</u> is for sale.

The girl <u>sitting next to me</u> is my cousin.

Adverb phrases add information about verbs:

He sat down <u>near the shed</u>. (tells us **where**)

It rained <u>all day</u>. (tells us **when**)

He lifted the box <u>with great difficulty</u>. (tells us **how**)

Look at how different phrases can be used to extend this simple sentence in three different ways: The dog buried the bone.

The dog <u>with the waggly tail</u> buried the bone. (adjective phrase)

The dog buried the bone <u>in our garden</u>. (adverb phrase telling us **where**)

The dog buried the bone <u>with great care</u>. (adverb phrase telling us **how**)

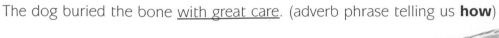

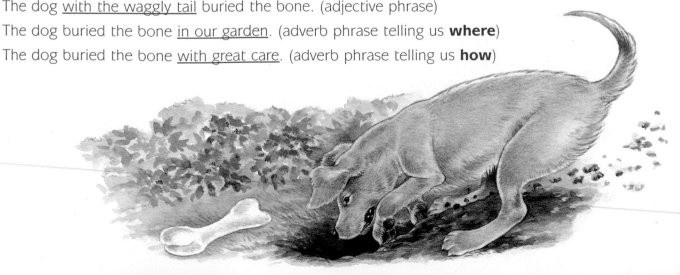

Clauses

A **clause** is a group of words which contains a verb. Clauses can be used to extend a sentence, and may be adjectival or adverbial.

Adjectival clauses often begin with *who*, *which*, *that*, *whose* or *whom*, and add information about nouns. Notice the use of commas to separate off the clause.

The girl, <u>who lives across the road</u>, is very generous.

The lady, <u>whose bag was stolen</u>, is very upset.

Adverbial clauses answer the questions *how? when? where?* or *why?* about the verb.

I'll meet you <u>where we met yesterday</u>. (tells us **where**)

He fell fast asleep <u>because he was tired</u>. (tells us **why**)

Look at how different clauses can be used to extend this simple sentence in three different ways: The boy arrived late.

The boy, <u>whose alarm clock did not go off</u>, arrived late. (adjectival clause)

The boy arrived late <u>because he stopped to watch fire fighters put out a fire</u>. (adverbial clause telling us why)

The boy, <u>who had lost his watch</u>, arrived late. (adjectival clause)

Test yourself

1 Find two different ways to make these sentences more interesting by adding phrases. Use a variety of different types.

   a The man fell.
   b The girl painted the door.
   c The cat chased the mouse.
   d The van parked outside.

2 Make these sentences more interesting in three different ways:

   ● by adding an adjectival clause;
   ● by adding an adverbial clause;
   ● by adding two different clauses.

   Remember to use commas where they are needed.

   a The man was very excited.
   b The girl wrote a letter.
   c The boy opened the window.
   d The road was flooded.

Answers and Guidance are given on p.41. *How long did you take?*

Answers and Guidance

Here is a chance for you to check your answers to the questions. Examples are given of possible ways of answering the questions and you should compare your answer.

1 Beginnings and endings

1 This is an example of a good beginning using speech:

> **"Now what's Scott Bulmer up to?" wondered Ravi.**
>
> **"No good, I expect," replied Saheed. Lying unseen in long grass, the two boys watched the school bully digging a hole under a tree.**
>
> **"Keep your head down," warned Ravi.**
>
> **"What's he doing?"**
>
> **"He's taken something out of his pocket and put it in the hole. Now he's filling the hole in."**
>
> **"Do you think it's stolen goods?" asked Saheed.**
>
> **"I wouldn't be surprised," replied Ravi. Suddenly he dropped flat to the ground. "Not a sound," he warned. "He's coming this way!"**

The 'hook' for the reader is the opening question. The conversation introduces us to Ravi and Saheed, but more importantly it tells us their opinion of Scott Bulmer. The speech is also used to describe what is happening; for example, "Not a sound," he warned. "He's coming this way!" Would you want to leave the story at this point?

Check your own work carefully to see if it hooks the reader, introduces characters and describes action.

2 Here is a good example of a surprise ending:

> **Jason climbed through a hole in the fence and began to cross the moonlit graveyard. Although this route saved him a long walk round, he was not as brave as he claimed. He always found that the darkness in the centre of the graveyard was rather frightening. That night there was a full moon which made shadows all around. Jason hurried on, his heart beginning to beat a little faster, and a little louder. As he reached the very centre, the moon slipped behind a cloud, and the graveyard was plunged into darkness.**
>
> **It was then that Jason had the fright of his life. From somewhere in front of him he heard a low moaning sound. He froze, still as stone. The moaning changed into a deep mocking laugh, growing louder until it echoed around the graveyard. Jason screamed. He raced towards the gate at the far end of the graveyard. As he**
> **stumbled through it, he almost crashed into Sam and Gary. Without a word, he hurried on down the street.**
>
> **"We're too late," said a disappointed Gary, carrying a portable tape recorder. "I told you we should have got here earlier."**
>
> **"He looked scared," said Sam. "Do you think he saw a ghost?"**
>
> **"No such thing," laughed Gary. But as they set off up the road they looked back at the gloomy graveyard.**

The writer of this ending has used the description of the graveyard, and Jason's increasing fear, to build the suspense. The ghostly sounds do not come as a shock because the reader is expecting them, but the ending is a complete surprise. Until the point where Jason almost crashes into Gary and Sam, we are led to believe that their plan to trick him has worked. Now we are left wondering if there is a real ghost in the graveyard. Ask an adult to read through your surprise ending with you.

 Target time for both questions: 25 minutes

 Your time for both questions |

2 Describing the setting

1 This is a good example of descriptive writing:

> **The sound of drums drew me to the street where the carnival was taking place. I could hear their pounding, like waves on the shore, many streets away. Then, as I turned the corner, I saw a blaze of colour and movement. Laughter mixed with the sound of music. People were dancing, in dazzling costumes of all the colours of the rainbow. The smell of spicy food made my mouth water. I joined in the celebration.**

The writer describes the scene using the senses of sight, sound, smell and taste. The description is also brought to life by a simile ('like waves on the shore'), a metaphor ('a blaze of colour and movement'), and powerful words such as 'pounding' and 'dazzling'.

Check your own description and your plan for it. Planning is an important part of writing and you will be expected to show planning in your National Test Writing paper. Did you find that your plan made your writing easier? Did it help to have a list of ideas to draw on?

Answers and Guidance

Check your finished description carefully. Does it create the right carnival atmosphere? Have you described its sights and sounds effectively? Have you used any of the other senses in your description? Have you described your thoughts and feelings about the carnival?

Look for special effects in your writing: powerful words, similes and metaphors. How do they help to create atmosphere? Can any of them be improved?

2 It is always easier to describe a place you know well. When selecting a question from your National Test Writing paper, always try to write about what you know. This will help to make your writing more real and interesting.

Read through your description carefully. Does it create the right atmosphere? Have you used three or more senses in your description? Have you described your thoughts and feelings? Are you happy with the language you have used? How might your work be improved?

 Target time for both questions: 30 minutes

 Your time for both questions [   ]

3 Creating believable characters

Session 1

1 This description shows the reader that the boy is timid by describing how he behaves and what he is thinking and feeling:

Josh was a very timid boy and the dog frightened him. There was no way round it so he decided to move very slowly, hoping not to disturb it. As he got near it the dog raised its head and looked him in the eye. Josh froze. He was sure the dog was going to attack him. He turned tail and ran away. The dog watched him disappear, and then went back to sleep.

Read through your own work carefully. Have you given enough description to help your reader imagine your character? Have you found a way of letting your reader know the boy is timid, without actually saying so?

2 Read through your description. Does it explain what the girl is thinking and feeling? Does it give any clues as to why she feels that way?

Target time for both questions: 15 minutes  **Your time** [   ]

3 Check your writing carefully. In your first paragraph you should have given your reader a few details about the boy's appearance and suggested what kind of person he is. In paragraph two you should have shown what he thinks and feels about going into the building site. What he does in paragraph three should be 'in character'. In other words, he should behave in a way the reader will expect from what has gone before. If you have done this your reader will understand your character and believe in his behaviour.

Ask an adult to go through your writing with you.

Target time: 20 minutes **Your time** [   ]

4 Using speech

Session 1

1 This is a good example of speech which reveals the characters and moves the plot along.

"I wonder what's in that box?" said Joe, pointing to an old wooden box floating in the canal.

"Let's find out," suggested Lee. "All we need is a long stick."

"Which we haven't got."

"There are trees all along here. There's bound to be something we can use."

"It's wrong to break branches off trees," warned Joe.

"Who said anything about breaking branches? Look, this will do fine." Lee pulled an old twig out of the long grass at the side of the tow path.

"It's not long enough."

"Of course it is." Lee stretched the stick at arm's length, but couldn't quite reach it. "Hold on to my other arm," he told Joe.

"I don't think this is a good idea," warned Joe, but when he held his friend's arm Lee was just able to reach the box.

The conversation begins with a question to which most readers will want to know the answer. The thoughts and feelings of the two characters show the differences between them: Joe is cautious, while Lee is willing to take risks to rescue the box. The writer makes clear who is speaking, and does not use unnecessary words.

Answers and Guidance

Check your own writing carefully. Does your dialogue tell your readers about the thoughts and feelings of the two children? Are there any unnecessary words? Have you used speech marks and other dialogue punctuation properly? Have you begun a new line for each speaker? Does the conversation move the plot along?

| Target time: 15 minutes | Your time | |

Session 2

2 Read through your writing carefully. Is it clear who is speaking? Does the conversation tell your readers the thoughts and feelings of the characters? Have you made every word count? Are there any unnecessary words?

Ask an adult to go through your writing with you.

| Target time: 15 minutes | Your time | |

5 Recipe for a story

Session 1

1 Here is a good example of how speech and description can be mixed with narrative without interrupting the flow of the story.

Nick and and his friend Tony were walking home from school. They passed a big stone house, with a high fence around its large gardens. Suddenly they heard children's laughter from behind the fence.

"I wonder what's going on in there," said Tony.

"Let's take a look," suggested Nick. They looked for a crack to look through, but there didn't seem to be any. Then Tony noticed a hole above their heads. It was big enough to see through if only they could reach it.

"If I stand on your shoulders," said Tony, "I'll be able to see what's going on."

"OK," agreed Nick, and he let his friend climb up to the hole. Peeping through, Tony could see two children about ten years old swimming in a large pool. They were really enjoying themselves.

"What can you see?" asked Nick.

"Shh! They might hear us," whispered Tony.

| Target time: 15 minutes | Your time | |

Session 2

2 How successfully do you think you have mixed description, dialogue and action? Can you think of ways to improve your 'recipe' for writing? Ask an adult to go through your writing with you.

| Target time: 15 minutes | Your time | |

6 Different ways to tell a story

Session 1

1 Here is a good beginning to the story of the girl and the spider:

There's not much I'm afraid of. I never worry about going to the dentist, even if it means a filling. The dentist's drill holds no fears for Katy Williams. But there is one thing that has me breaking out into a cold sweat, and that's spiders. There's something about all those legs and the way they move that makes me curl up screaming. And that's where my story begins.

It was half past eight, and I was late for school. As I dashed towards my bedroom door I saw it hanging there: a huge hairy spider lowering itself on a thread in front of the doorway, blocking my escape.

The opening introduces us to Katy, and tells the reader that she is not really a coward, just someone afraid of spiders.

| Target time: 15 minutes | Your time | |

Session 2

2 This is a good opening to the science-fiction story about time travel:

The sign in the amusement dome wasn't really there. You could walk right through its glowing letters. But the time travel adventure it promised was real enough.

"Travel through time," it read. "Any place, any time you like."

"Let's do it!" exclaimed Nik.

"OK," agreed Tami. They handed over the 20 credits admission and went into a small dark room.

"Please sit down," said a voice. Two comfortable seats glowed for a few moments in the centre of the room. Nik and Tami sat down.

"Don't be nervous," the voice comforted them. "We guarantee a safe, but exciting, adventure. Now where and when would you like to go?"

It is told in the third person. It includes the technology of a sci-fi story: a hologram sign you can walk through and, of course, a time machine.

| Target time: 15 minutes | Your time | |

7 Paragraphs and headings

Session 1

1 Here is a plan for writing about penguins. It uses a main heading, sub-headings and brief notes.

Penguins
What they look like
Flightless birds – stout bodies, short legs – black above and white below – wings like flippers – body covered with short feathers. Swim underwater powerfully.
Where they live
Colder waters south of equator. Some breed in Antarctica.
What they eat
Fish, squid.
Their young
Gather together to breed. Female lays single egg in May – goes to sea to feed – male sits on egg for two months without eating. Female then cares for newly hatched chick – male goes to sea for food. Many chicks die from storms or are eaten by other birds and animals.

Your finished writing should have a suitable main heading (e.g. the name of your chosen creature), and then a short paragraph for each of the sub-headings above.

| Target time: 20 minutes | 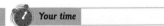 Your time | |

Session 2

2 This is a good example of a short plan, with sub-headings, for writing about football.

Football
Short introduction: most popular game in world
Equipment
What is needed

Rules
Short explanation of how to play
Why football is so popular
Why people enjoy playing and watching it.

Check your own work. Your plan should have headings and brief descriptions of the main ideas, like the one above. Check the layout of your finished writing. Have you used appropriate headings and sub-headings? Do your headings and sub-headings tell the main idea of each paragraph? Does your last paragraph bring your writing to an effective ending?

| Target time: 20 minutes | Your time | |

8 Different ways to organise your writing

Session 1

1 This is a good example of a leaflet on protecting a park. It is aimed at local children and adults.

Protect our Park

Spring Lea Park is under threat. Join our campaign to save it.

- Vandals are damaging the swings and other equipment in the children's play area. These have had to be repaired several times, which is very expensive. If this damage continues, the play area may have to be closed for good.
- Litter is a big problem in Spring Lea. Although there are lots of litter bins, many people are too lazy to use them. Broken bottles are a big problem.
- Too many dog owners are failing to clean up the dog mess when they take their dogs for walks. This makes many paths and grassy areas too dirty to walk on.
- Gates are being left wide open, and many are now off their hinges because children swing on them.
- The fences around the sports area have holes in several places. Children climb through and play on the new running track. The track has been damaged.

Act now to save your park:
- Report any vandalism you see.
- Put litter in the bins.
- Clean up after your dogs.
- Close gates, and never climb through or over fences.
- Write to the council and the *Bloggstown News* to let them know you care about the park.

Spring Lea is a beautiful park. If we all work to protect it we can keep it that way.

Answers and Guidance

Check your own work. Does it meet its purpose? Will your intended readers understand it? Did you cover all the important points? Is your presentation attractive and eye-catching? Do you think your work will persuade your readers to protect the park?

Target time: 25 minutes | **Your time** |

Session 2

2 Is your leaflet suitable for children 5–8 years old? Will they understand it? Have you avoided using difficult words and long sentences? Do you think it will persuade them to be careful about fireworks? Have you included some headings?

Ask an adult to go through your writing with you.

Target time: 20 minutes | **Your time** |

9 Covering the important points

Session 1

1 Here is a good sample letter about the school trip. Compare yours with this.

Dear Parent,

Class 6 will be going on a trip to Malham on Thursday 12 June. We will be travelling by coach.

The trip is part of our project on water. We will walk from the car park at Malham to Malham Cove, where we will have a packed lunch. Then we will take the path to Malham Tarn. The coach will pick us up there at 4.00 pm. We expect to be back at school at about 6.00 pm.

The cost of the trip works out at £5.00 per pupil. Please can this be brought into school as soon as possible. The children will need to have waterproof clothing, a back pack and a packed lunch.

Please complete and return the permissions slip by Friday 9 May.

Yours faithfully,

S. Brown (class teacher)

Target time: 15 minutes | **Your time** |

Session 2

2 Your brochure plan might use some of these headings:

Welcome to _____ School (introduction welcoming new pupils)

School hours
Uniform
School meals
Sports
School clubs
School rules

Ask an adult to read through the notes you have made under each heading.

Target time: 10 minutes | 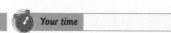 **Your time** |

Session 3

3 Check the points you have made under each heading. Have you missed out anything important? Ask an adult to go through them with you.

Target time: 15 minutes | **Your time** |

10 Writing a good conclusion

Session 1

1 This is a sample plan for 'Is watching TV a waste of time?'.

<u>Introduction</u>
Most people watch TV. Some watch many hours a week – are they wasting their time?
<u>Why watching TV is a good idea</u>
Up-to-date news
Can learn about lots of things
Watching sports and films is cheaper on TV
Need to sit down and relax
<u>Why watching TV is a waste of time</u>
Time spent watching TV could be used for doing things: going out, reading
Children who watch too much TV are not very healthy
People spend time at home instead of meeting others
Too much violence
<u>Conclusion</u>
Good as long as it's not too much each day

Answers and Guidance

This is a good conclusion which gives an opinion:

Too much TV can be bad for you as it stops you doing other things. I think you need to choose the programmes you watch carefully. If you do this, you can learn about interesting things and still have time to play sport and read.

Target time: 20 minutes | Your time

Session 2

2 Does your conclusion summarise the main reasons why your chosen room is your favourite? Ask an adult to go through your writing with you.

Target time: 20 minutes | Your time

11 Choosing the right language

Session 1

1 and **2** Check each piece of your writing in turn. Is the language and vocabulary appropriate to its type, purpose and audience?

Target time for both questions: 25 minutes | Your time

Session 2

These are good examples of two different descriptions of the same school. Note the choice of language, purpose and audience. Go through your own writing with an adult and decide how well you have chosen your own language.

3 An article for a local newspaper about interesting local buildings:

Danby School was built in 1926. The date is carved into one of the stones of the entrance pillars on Victoria St. The school has two floors and is built in an 'L' shape. The lower windows have arches, but the upper windows are rectangular. The red brick walls are now dirty. There are twelve classrooms. They all look out onto the playground and playing field. From the upper floor, there are views of the hills. The people who built Danby School chose a good spot.

4 The opening paragraph of 'The Mystery of Danby School':

In the moonlight, the children saw a shadow slip along the school's dirty red brick walls. For a moment, the shadow stopped at the upstairs window of Class 6. Then it slid down to the arched windows of Class 3. Then it stopped again. The children watched as it moved out onto the playing field, and disappeared into the hills.

Notice how the newspaper article lists the interesting features of the building. It is full of facts. It describes the arched windows, stone pillars and 'L-shaped building.

The opening to the story describes the same building differently. Here it is the moonlit setting for a mystery story. The writer has carefully chosen the language. The writer has selected only the details of the school which help describe the movement of the shadow: the dirty brick walls, the arched windows, the hills.

Target time: 25 minutes | Your time

12 Using similes and metaphors

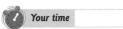

1
- **a** metaphor
- **b** simile
- **c** metaphor
- **d** simile
- **e** metaphor
- **f** metaphor
- **g** simile
- **h** simile.

2 These are examples of suitable similes and metaphors. Decide whether yours are as good.

- **a** Clouds raced across the sky <u>like frightened sheep</u>.
- **b** The stone statue was <u>silver</u> in the moonlight.
- **c** The wind tore at his clothes <u>like icy fingers</u>.
- **d** In winter the house is <u>a fridge</u>.
- **e** Getting my brother to change his mind is <u>like trying to swim through</u> <u>treacle</u>.
- **f** When it comes to remembering things my sister is <u>an elephant</u>.

3 This example uses similes and metaphors well. Compare your own writing with this.

Jan swam through the clear water, a mermaid in the blue sea. The tropical fish were brightly coloured jewels. They flashed before Jan's eyes, but then were gone.

Target time for all questions: 20 minutes | Your time

Answers and Guidance

13 Punctuating speech

Session 1

1 **"Doctor, I think I'm a pair of curtains!" said the patient.**

"Pull yourself together," replied the doctor.

"Waiter," said the diner, "there's a twig in my soup."

"Hold on," replied the waiter, "I'll call the branch manager."

2 Use the rules on page 28 to check that you have used speech marks and other punctuation correctly.

3 This version of the dialogue uses all the rules shown on page 28. Find an example of the use of each rule.

"Ben, help Dad with the washing up," said Mum.

"But, Mum," protested Ben, "it's Carly's turn today."

"Carly, as you well know, has got to go back to school," pointed out Mum.

"But, I did the dishes last night," whined Ben, "and tomorrow night Carly is going to Auntie Helen's for tea."

"Then she'll have to wash the dishes two nights running," replied Mum.

"It'll be three nights running," said Ben.

"Will it?" asked Mum. She looked puzzled and then said, "I'll have to think about that one. Now help your dad."

"It's all right," called Dad from the kitchen. "I've finished."

Target time for all questions: 15 minutes Your time [ ]

Session 2

4 Use the rules on page 28 to check that you have used speech marks and other punctuation correctly.

Target time: 15 minutes Your time [ ]

14 More punctuation

1 These are the words you should have used in your sentences:

a the man's hammer   d the drivers' cars

b Ms Smith's car   e the painters' brushes

c the girls' coats   f the girl's pens.

Make sure the other punctuation in your sentences is correct: check your use of full stops, commas and capital letters.

2 These are the shortened forms you should have used in your sentences:

a shouldn't   d it's

b we're   e they've

c you'll   f won't

Note that it's is short for 'it is', whereas its means 'belonging to it'.

3 These are examples of sentences with colons. Compare yours with these.

a The most popular activities included: scuba diving, rock climbing, deep-sea fishing and hang-gliding.

b The chocolate melted: Harry had left it in the sun.

4 Here are examples of the use of dashes. Compare yours with these.

a Liam is captain – no, he's had his turn already.

b The last thing to remember – and this is very important – is never return to a lighted firework.

5 These are two examples of the use of brackets. Compare yours with these.

a The masked figure (Sam in disguise) crept towards the door.

b James insisted he was in bed with the flu (even though Lisa saw him playing football).

Target time for all questions: 15 minutes  Your time [ ]

Answers and Guidance

15 Making sentences more interesting

1 These are examples of how you could make the sentences more interesting by using phrases. Compare your sentences with these.

a The man <u>on the cliff</u> fell.
The man fell <u>with a loud cry</u>.

b The girl painted the door <u>at the side of the house</u>.
The girl <u>with red hair</u> painted the door.

c The cat chased the mouse <u>into a hole</u>.
The cat <u>without a tail</u> chased the mouse.

d The van parked outside <u>all day</u>.
The van <u>with the scratch down the side</u> parked outside.

2 These are examples of how the sentences can be made more interesting by using clauses. Compare your sentences with these.

a The man <u>who had won the lottery</u> was very excited. (adjectival clause)
The man was very excited <u>because his son had passed his exams</u>. (adverbial clause)
The man <u>who came first in the race</u> was very excited <u>because he had never run so fast before</u>.

b The girl, <u>who had just learned to use a pen</u>, wrote a letter. (adjectival clause)
The girl wrote a letter <u>as soon as she arrived home from school</u>. (adverbial clause)
The girl, <u>whose birthday it was</u>, wrote a letter <u>to thank her Aunty for sending her a present</u>.

c The boy, <u>who had seen his friend outside</u>, opened the window. (adjectival clause)
The boy opened the window <u>although it was a cold day</u>. (adverbial clause)
The boy, <u>who was frightened of the wasp</u>, opened the window <u>so that it would fly out again</u>.

d The road <u>which ran through the village</u> was flooded. (adjectival clause)
The road was flooded <u>by the time James arrived</u>. (adverbial clause)
The road, <u>which was close to the river</u>, was flooded <u>when it overflowed its banks</u>.

Target time for all questions: 15 minutes   **Your time**

Choose one piece of writing from the four listed below:

1   **'Autumn Adventure'** – a short story

2   **'Elephant in the Garden'** – a short story

3   **'Keep the Playground'** – a leaflet

4   **'Dear Bored'** – a letter.

Allow yourself 15 minutes to think and plan what you want to write. If you choose to write a story, make brief notes on the story planning sheet (page 44) to help you plan your ideas. Remember to plan:

- How the story begins and ends.
- What the setting is (where and when does the story take place).
- Who the characters are and what they are like.
- What happens (the plot).

Give yourself 45 minutes to do your writing.

1 'Autumn Adventure'

Write an adventure or mystery story set in autumn. Include descriptions of the colours, sights and sounds of autumn.

You should think about:
- who is telling the story;
- who else is in the story;
- what happens;
- how it will end.

2 'Elephant in the Garden'

> For a brief moment the whole room was silent as I announced what I could see, and then the chaos began.

Start your story with these words. Then continue your story by writing about what happened next.

Try to get the fun and excitement of 'What do we do with an elephant in our garden?' into your story to amuse and grip your reader.

3 'Keep the Playground'

There are plans to put a new road through the local playground. If this goes through, there will be nowhere safe for children to play.

Your task is to prepare a leaflet to encourage people to join you in raising objections.

Remember your readers will want to know:
- the important facts about the plans;
- what they can do to give support: meetings, letters, petitions.

New Road Through Play Area
Plans published today show a new road going through the Valley Playground. Work is expected to start on Tuesday

Valley News

Another near miss
Last week, for the second time this month a child just missed adding to the death toll on our roads. Sam Green, aged 9, chased his ball into the road and was narrowly missed by a large lorry.

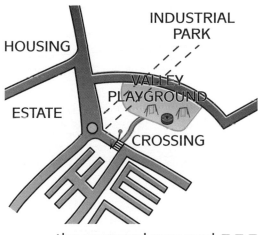

the proposed new road = = =

Residents in Uproar
"Children first", say local residents over plans for a new road. Parents in the Valley area are protesting in an effort to save the children's playground. They will be writing to the Council, holding meetings and preparing a petition.

4 'Dear Bored'

A letter has appeared in your local newspaper from someone new to the area. In it they complain that there is nothing to do. They say that your area must be one of the most boring in the whole country.

Write a letter in response which:
- points out all the leisure facilities and activities that are available;
- encourages your readers to give them a try.

Answers and Guidance

National Test: Writing

Story writing: 'Autumn Adventure' or 'Elephant in the Garden'

You need to decide what level your story would probably be awarded if you had written it in the National Test. To do this you need to read through the statements below and tick those that you feel apply to your story.

These statements are similar to the criteria that the Test Markers use when marking the Writing Test paper.

The statements are at three different levels: Level 3, Level 4 and Level 5. To achieve Level 4, you must be able to tick all, or most, of the Level 4 statements, as well as all those for Level 3. To achieve Level 5, you must be able to tick all, or most, of the Level 5 statements, as well as all those for Levels 3 and 4.

Share the checking of your story with an adult.

Level 3

Purpose and organisation	Yes
The events in my story are organised with a beginning, a middle and an end.	
The events are in a sensible order.	
I have linked the events by using language such as 'one day', 'suddenly' and 'then'.	
I have used words such as 'but', 'when', 'so' and 'because' to link ideas in sentences.	
I have added interest to my story by including a simple setting and/or brief description of character.	

Grammar (Punctuation and style)	Yes
I have used capital letters and full stops to mark at least half my sentences.	
I have used question marks and/or exclamation marks accurately.	
I have sometimes tried to show speech by using inverted commas.	
Within sentences, subjects and verbs usually agree.	
I have used and spelt correctly simple adjectives and adverbs (e.g. 'fiery leaves', 'running quickly').	

If you can say 'yes' to most of these statements and tick them, then your writing is within Level 3.

Level 4

To award your writing Level 4, you need to be able to tick all or most of the statements below, as well as the Level 3 ones.

Purpose and organisation	Yes
My first paragraph is interesting and sets the scene.	
My last paragraph rounds off the story successfully.	
I have used a new paragraph when introducing a change of place, time, character or event.	
I have described my characters quite fully so that the reader can get to know them.	
The people behave 'in character' and/or change because of an event.	
I have included dialogue and my characters talk in the way that they would in real life.	

Grammar (Punctuation and style)	Yes
I have remembered to put speech on a new line.	
I have used capital letters, commas, full stops, question marks and exclamation marks correctly.	
I have used apostrophes when abbreviating words or when someone owns something.	
Some of the verbs I have used have an adverb to describe them.	
Verb tenses are generally consistent throughout.	
I have included some complex sentences using a variety of different connecting words (e.g. 'if' 'however', 'although').	
I have tried to use imaginative and exciting words in my descriptions (e.g. a 'nice' day would be a 'glorious' day, and a 'nice' game would be an 'exciting' game).	

Answers and Guidance

If you can say 'yes' to most of these statements and tick them, then your writing is within Level 4.

Level 5

To award your writing Level 5, you need to be able to tick all or most of the statements below, as well as the Level 3 and Level 4 ones.

Purpose and organisation	Yes
My writing has a clear and consistent form to it (e.g. realistic narrative, fable, adventure etc.).	
I have used speech or action to begin my first paragraph to encourage the reader to read on.	
I have used paragraphing to build up the suspense or make my reader wait for a surprise.	
There is interaction between my characters and they influence the plot.	
The language that my main characters use tells the reader something about them.	
The way I have written the descriptive passages means that the reader can get a clear picture of the setting or place.	
I have interwoven speech (dialogue), action and description in my story.	
I have included comments on the thoughts and feelings of my characters.	
I have shown that I can bring a twist to the ending or end my story in another equally satisfying way.	

Grammar (Punctuation and style)	Yes
I have used commas correctly within sentences to separate clauses, phrases or items in a list.	
I have included a variety of simple and complex sentences to add interest to my writing.	
I have used a range of punctuation correctly.	
My writing uses interesting and imaginative vocabulary and the language I have chosen conveys clearly what I want to say.	
Overall, my style of writing holds the interest and attention of the reader.	
I have included some complex sentences using a variety of different connecting words (e.g. 'if', 'however', 'although').	

If you can say 'yes' to most of these statements and tick them, then you are within Level 5.

How to improve your story writing

Now that you have looked closely at your story you may find it helpful to look back at some of the chapters in this book (and *Success in English Book 2*) to see if you can improve on certain things.

Was the beginning of your story strong enough to make your reader want to read on?

CROSS-CHECK CHAPTER 1 Beginnings and endings

Did your story have a surprising or other satisfying ending?

CROSS-CHECK CHAPTER 1 Beginnings and endings

Did you describe the setting in detail? Did you create atmosphere by the way you used language?

CROSS-CHECK CHAPTER 2 Describing the setting
CHAPTER 12 Using similes and metaphors

Did you create believable characters? Did you describe their thoughts and feelings? Did they always speak and behave 'in character'?

CROSS-CHECK CHAPTER 3 Creating believable characters

Did you use speech well? Did you use it to show what your characters were like and to move the plot along? Did you punctuate it correctly?

CROSS-CHECK CHAPTER 4 Using speech
CHAPTER 13 Punctuating speech

Did you tell your story consistently in the first person or the third person?

CROSS-CHECK CHAPTER 6 Different ways to tell a story

Did you decide on a suitable form for your story? For example, if you chose 'Autumn Adventure' did you include enough of the 'ingredients' of an adventure story?

CROSS-CHECK CHAPTER 6 Different ways to tell a story

Did you use a good mix of narrative, speech and description in your story?

CROSS-CHECK CHAPTER 5 A recipe for a story

Did you include a variety of interesting sentences?

CROSS-CHECK CHAPTER 15 Making sentences more interesting

You could decide to redraft your story to include improvements, or you could try the other story writing task to see if you can do better the second time around.

Answers and Guidance

Information writing: 'Keep the Playground' (leaflet) or 'Dear Bored' (letter)

You need to decide what level your information writing would probably be awarded if you had written it in the National Test. To do this you need to read through the statements below and tick those that you feel apply to your writing.

These statements are similar to the criteria that the Test Markers use when marking the Writing Test paper.

The statements are at three different levels: Level 3, Level 4 and Level 5. To achieve Level 4, you must be able to tick all, or most, of the Level 4 statements, as well as all those for Level 3. To achieve Level 5, you must be able to tick all, or most, of the Level 5 statements, as well as all those for Levels 3 and 4.

Share the checking of your writing with an adult.

Level 3

Purpose and organisation	Yes
In the leaflet, I have given some thought to layout by including headings.	
In the letter, I have included correctly most of the features you would expect to see (e.g. address, date, greeting etc.).	
I have made my points in a sensible order although I have not included very many different ones.	
It is clear from my writing when I am expressing personal opinions.	
I have given some detail through description.	

Grammar (Punctuation and style)	Yes
I have used capital letters and full stops to mark at least half my sentences.	
I have used some other punctuation correctly (e.g. question mark, exclamation mark).	
I have used simple adjectives and adverbs and spelt them correctly.	

If you can say 'yes' to most of these statements and tick them, then your writing is within Level 3.

Level 4

To award your writing Level 4, you need to be able to tick most of the statements below, as well as the Level 3 ones.

Purpose and organisation	Yes
My first paragraph sets the scene and introduces the subject.	
My final paragraph concludes my writing effectively.	
The middle section of my letter mentions the various facilities and activities in an interesting and detailed way.	
The layout of my leaflet helps the reader with headings, sub-titles and new paragraphs for each main point.	
My writing is convincing. It would encourage future support ('Keep the Playground') or would convince readers to try out the leisure facilities ('Dear Bored').	

Grammar (Punctuation and style)	Yes
I have used capital letters, commas, full stops, question marks and exclamation marks correctly.	
I have used apostrophes when abbreviating words or when someone owns something.	
Some of the verbs I have used have an adverb to describe them.	
My verb tenses are generally consistent throughout.	
I have included some complex sentences using a variety of different connecting words (e.g. 'if', 'however', 'although').	
I have used a style that is suitable for my audience – i.e. to persuade my readers of the problem ('Keep the Playground') or to describe the many things there are to do ('Dear Bored').	

If you can say 'yes' to most of these statements and tick them, then your writing is within Level 4.

Answers and Guidance

Level 5

To award your writing Level 5, you need to be able to tick most of the statements below, as well as the Level 3 and 4 ones.

Purpose and organisation	Yes
The purpose of my writing is clear right from the very beginning.	
The information is laid out in a way that helps the reader to understand the facts fully.	
The tone of my writing is appropriate (i.e. formal) and convincing but with some personal opinions included.	
I have covered all the topics that should be included in the appropriate depth.	
I have used paragraphs or sub-headings to mark the main sections (leaflet).	

Grammar (Punctuation and style)	Yes
I have used commas correctly within sentences to separate clauses, phrases or items in a list.	
I have included a wide range of punctuation correctly.	
I have used technical and specific words where appropriate.	
Overall, my piece is written in such a way that it really will encourage my readers to voice their objections to the plan ('Keep the Playground') or to try out the leisure facilities ('Dear Bored').	

If you can answer 'yes' to most of these statements and tick them, then you are within Level 5.

How to improve your information writing

Now that you have looked closely at your information writing, you may find it helpful to look back at some of the chapters in this book to see if you can improve on certain things.

Did you organise your information sensibly? Did you include paragraphs with headings in your leaflet and paragraphs in your letter?

CROSS-CHECK **CHAPTER 7** Paragraphs and headings

Does your leaflet/letter fit its purpose and audience? Is the language you chose suitable?

CROSS-CHECK **CHAPTER 8** Different ways to organise your writing
CHAPTER 11 Choosing the right language

Did you plan your writing first to ensure that you covered all the important points?

CROSS-CHECK **CHAPTER 9** Covering the main points

Did you write an effective last paragraph?

CROSS-CHECK **CHAPTER 10** Writing a good conclusion

Did you use a range of different puntuation?

CROSS-CHECK **CHAPTER 14** More punctuation

Now that you have looked closely at your writing, you may find it helpful to redraft it by making improvements. You might, on the other hand, decide to try the other information writing task to see if you can do even better the second time around.